To: My Auntie Sadie

Love
From: your Hailey Baby

MERRY CHRISTMAS 2010
XOXOXOXOX

LOTS OF LOVE AND HAPPINESS
THROUGH OUT THE NEW YEAR!

Have Yourself a Beary Little Christmas

The Boyds Collection Ltd.®

Text written by Patrick Regan

**Andrews McMeel
Publishing**

Kansas City

Have Yourself a Beary Little Christmas

For information, write Andrews McMeel Publishing, an Andrews McMeel Universal company,
4520 Main Street, Kansas City, Missouri 64111.

04 05 06 07 08 WKT 10 9 8 7 6 5 4 3 2 1

ISBN: 0-7407-4681-2

Library of Congress Control Number: 2004102687

Book design by Holly Camerlinck

Have Yourself a
Beary Little Christmas

Brrr . . . There's a chill in the air.

And folks are hustling and
bustling everywhere.

Children are being very, very good.

And—if you listen closely—
you just might hear the faint sound
of sleigh bells in the distance.

Ah . . . there's no mistaking it—
it's Christmastime once again!

And there's no time

quite like Christmas,

When stars shine bright
in clear, wintry skies,

Houses fill with the enticing aroma
of fresh-baked holiday treats,

Old friends stop by
to share good cheer,

And we're reminded how good it
feels to give of ourselves.

At Christmas, *everyone* seems to be

just a tad more merry.

Christmas is a time to embrace

longtime traditions

And create fun new ones.

It's a time for favorite old ornaments

And fuzzy new sweaters,

For singing carols door-to-door

And frolicking in the snow

on a frosty morning.

It's a time to deck the halls—
and ourselves—
in full holiday finery.

And—
whether there's mistletoe or not—
Christmas is a great time
to say, "I love you."

Everyone looks forward to Christmas,
but for little ones the wait can
seem unbearable.

As the big day grows closer,
it gets harder and harder
to think about anything else!

Sometimes, kids get downright crazy
with anticipation!

Luckily, there's lots
to keep them occupied,

Like sledding,

Snowman making

And school programs where every
kid gets a chance to shine.

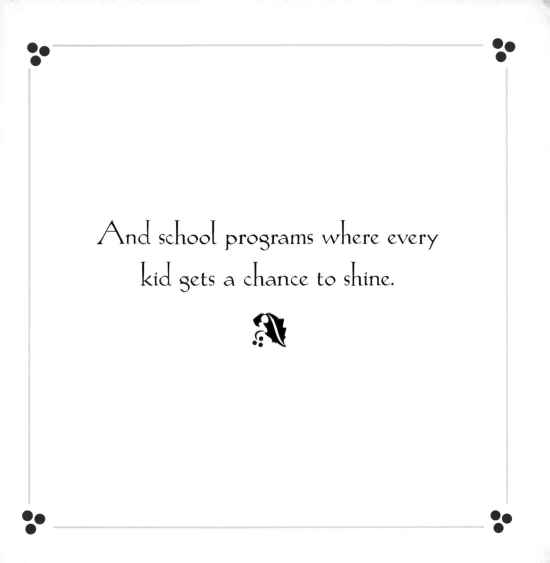

At fancy holiday parties, kids try hard to stay on their best behavior. (After all, *he* knows if you've been bad or good.)

It seems Christmas has a magical way
of bringing out the best in everyone.

(Maybe that's the work of
Christmas angels.)

As Christmas nears, kids daydream
about Santa tending his team
and loading his sleigh.

They wonder just what those elves
at the North Pole are working on

And what delightful surprises
might fill their stockings
on Christmas morning!

And when they *finally* shuffle off
to bed on Christmas Eve, all their
dreams revolve around one thing:

The Big Guy himself!

Yes, Christmas is for children—
children from one to ninety-two.

Because no matter how old we are,
there will always be magic and
wonder in Christmas . . . so long as
we believe in it with all our hearts.

Have yourself a
beary little Christmas!